Travels Through Burgundy

TRAVELS THROUGH BURGUNDY

Paintings by Margaret Loxton

Foreword by Alan Coren

PAVILION

First published in Great Britain in 1991 by
PAVILION BOOKS LIMITED
196 Shaftesbury Avenue, London WC2H 8JL

Designed by Bet Ayer

A CIP catalogue record for this book is available from
the British Library

ISBN: 1 85145 783 6

10 9 8 7 6 5 4 3 2 1

Printed and bound in Italy by New Interlitho

Frontispiece: Château Corton-André, Aloxe-Corton.

Foreword

Let me impress you. I knew about Burgundy when I was eleven.

I did not, however, know what it was. I knew only what it wasn't. I knew that it wasn't whalemeat rissoles and dehydrated potato and powdered egg. I knew that it wasn't Wincarnis and Haliborange and Camp Coffee. I knew that it wasn't sweet coupons and bread units and a piece of scrag if you were lucky enough to know the butcher. I knew, in short, that whatever Burgundy was, it wasn't austerity.

I knew this because in 1949, I saw *Passport to Pimlico*. Greatest of all the great Ealing comedies, this took as its nub the joyous conceit that, in the grey and wasted centre of post-war London, bombed-out, dreary, broke, cold, hungry, an ancient charter is unearthed proving Pimlico to be part of Burgundy. Whereupon, Pimlico instantly secedes from the United Kingdom and, marching behind the irrepressible leadership of Stanley Holloway, embraces its colonial birthright. It becomes Burgundy. Overnight, plenitude replaces austerity, and, freed from rationing, planning restrictions, licensing laws, and all the rest of 1949's bleak infibulations, the downtrodden wretches of Pimlico burst into the broad sunny uplands of a notional Côte d'Or, and *joie de vivre* is born. They become Burgundians.

As the closing credits rolled, I stumbled out into the drizzled gloaming of a bleak London afternoon, and trudged home for spam fritters, tapioca, and a bottle of the '49 cod-liver oil which my mother would broach for special occasions, i.e. when the day's diet appeared to be more than usually conducive to rickets. That night, I dreamed of Burgundy.

The dream, like many another pre-pubescent fantasy, wrought its wily conditioning upon the reality against which it was subsequently to be measured; however, unlike a fair few of the rest, it did not – when, a few years on, the dreamer came to tempt providence – leave reality wanting.

The execution immeasurably outstripped the anticipation.

That is the edge which gluttony has over lust.

Is, then, Burgundy sinful? Well, yes for those who refuse to see its gloriously uninhibited self-indulgence as a celebration of not merely life, but something more than life. The rest of us prefer to regard Burgundy as a huge natural cathedral whose devoted congregation is committed to the principle that if you're entering into communion with God, the first thing to ensure is that the bread and the wine are as close to divine as mortal man can make them. Furthermore, not only have no people on God's earth done more to nurture, cherish, and worship the blessings of that earth than the people of Burgundy, but, believe me, no-one is ever more truly grateful for what he has received than the bloke who has tied on the Burgundian bib.

Those who consider all this immoderate scoffing to be sinful, of course, will insist that Burgundy's unparalleled abundance of magnificent churches and cathedrals should be attributed not – as we others insist – to gratitude, but to guilt. To such spoilsports, I would concede only that guilt does indeed attach to such places, but it is as innocent a guilt as you could shake a censer at; and it racks, moreover, the consciences not of Burgundians but of those whose necessarily brief visits saddle them with hapless choices.

Take, for example, that most spectacular exemplar of Romanesque glory, the Abbey of St Philibert at Tournus, within easy walking distance of both the Restaurant Greuze and the Restaurant Le Rempart – but only for those who find walking easy. This inevitably excludes anyone who, having forked down three hours worth of *pâté en croute Alexandre Dumaine, salade de langoustines rôties aux pois gourmands, filet d'agneau en feuilles de riz, crêpes en millefeuille aux pommes et oranges* and sent all this stuff packing in the company of the best that the neighbouring slopes of Meursault and Macon can tread, suddenly finds himself unable to lift his guidebook, let alone act upon its recommendations.

Or take the quite astonishing Hotel-Dieu des Hospices de Beaune, which some would claim to be the most beautiful medieval building in the

world; an assertion with which I should be only too happy to concur, had I
not been incessantly sidetracked by the Hostellerie de Levernois just up the
road. You would not think, would you, that an architecture buff like me
would allow himself to be thwarted by *petits escargots en cocotte lutée*,
écrevisses au gratin, *poulet de Bresse rôti* and a couple of bottles of
Bourgogne Aligoté, but there you are, suddenly it's four o'clock and there's
time for nothing but a quick zizz before dinner.

For in Burgundy, I'm afraid, eyes – unlike the more fortunate bits – are
often doomed to remain unfeasted.

Which is just one of the myriad reasons why I rejoice in Margaret
Loxton's incomparable paintings. They offer me not only what I have seen,
but what I have missed. More even than that, they offer me what I have
missed in what I have seen. Most of all, they express that rapturous
celebration of fecundity which is uniquely Burgundian, and they express it
with a passion and a richness and a comic gusto which is itself an
embodiment of what it seeks to represent.

And still, within all this, there is a singularly English flavour, a relish in
the very *differentness* of what is observed, a note struck by the love of
something recognised as more exotic than itself.

I heard Stanley Holloway laugh like that, once upon a time.

ALAN COREN
London 1991

Gambling on good harvest weather, I chose cycling as the ideal means of transport for this journey. Cycling is quiet, understated, pollution free – and peasant friendly. The rhythm is gentle and relaxed, and being raised off the ground makes it easier to appreciate the finer details of the countryside.

Leaving Dijon, travelling south, I began my journey proper after the suburb of Chenove, following the signs for the 'Route des Grands Crus' – a road that winds its way on to the gentle slopes of the Côtes de Nuits and to the first of the great wine villages of Burgundy, Gevrey-Chambertin.

The old village of Gevrey-Chambertin lies at the foot of a picturesque, steep, short valley. Along either side of its narrow streets, behind high walls covered with ivy and wisteria, there are weathered old houses with outbuildings where the farmers make their wine – the main occupation of the village.

Côte de Nuits Vineyard

This was my first glimpse of wine harvesters since leaving Dijon. The vineyard is on the lower slopes of the Côte d'Or, and we are looking up at the 'Route des Grands Crus' and the famous villages nestling on the hillside.

Gevrey-Chambertin

I chose this particular view because it features the château built by the monks of Cluny in 1257. It is a reminder that the monastic orders were a major influence in the region and were responsible for establishing many of the vineyards that flourish today.

I liked the perspective of the view stretching outward from the tower of the château. Conditions were perfect. The light was clear, the colours vibrant and sharp. The vineyard workers moved rhythmically along the rows of vines.

Three Ladies of Gevrey-Chambertin

The remarkable success in recent years of the small *vignerons* of the Côte d'Or, who produce some of the world's best wine, is due in no small measure to the formidable practical skills of the wives of these farmers: three of whom stand here by the vineyard gates. They help with the harvest and keep meticulous vintage records, make careful note of cellar stocks and deal with supplies and sales.

MMLoxton

Judging the Wine: the Expert

For Jean-Jacques, one of the most distinguished and dedicated growers of Gevrey-Chambertin, vine cultivation is an organic process, demanding all his extensive knowledge, instinct and professionalism from winter pruning through spring tending to hand-picking the grapes. Adhering to time-honoured methods, he makes his *grand cru* wines in a simple village cellar, using new oak barrels for fermentation, though the wine press is modern. A celebrated Paris chef describes Jean-Jacques' wine as 'having every quality that a great Burgundy should possess'.

The Café Bar: The Bachelor Brothers

Two bachelor brothers sit a little weary and taciturn in a café at the end of a day's
unremarkable labours, tending their vines on their inherited farm on the lower
village slopes. They are resigned to their changeless wine-growing routine and to
selling the grapes to those with more expertise and ambition. Yet they are not
without contentment in their quiet way of life.

Clos St-Jacques

The Clos St-Jaques was founded by medieval monks forming a boundary
established after tireless experimentation, around one great vineyard. The wine
produced from grapes inside the walled enclosure is of the highest quality and
much sought after. Many such Clos, with their lovely weathered stone walls
forming abstract designs over the undulating terrain can be found throughout the
Côte d'Or.

In medieval Burgundy, the Church and the monasteries played a more
important role than any other region of France. They held extraordinary power
within the Duchy and their vineyard holdings were only rivalled by the nobility.

It was the French Revolution that broke up these huge estates. The priceless
land was sold to the tenant farmers and became family holdings. These lands were
further divided by the Napoleonic laws of succession, which overturned the old
laws of exclusive inheritance by the eldest son (primogeniture) in favour of
splitting the proceeds equally between all the children.

During the twentieth century the more ambitious small farmers who made and
marketed their own wine – becoming famous in the process – formed business
ventures to avoid further dispersal of the land through inheritance.

A short distance after Gevrey-
Chambertin is the village of Morey-
Saint-Denis. There is an air of quiet
enchantment about the village with its
wide main street and substantial
medieval and Renaissance courtyards,
mellow stone houses and vines
coming right up to the roadside.

Boules, Morey-Saint-Denis

Among the many considerable
pleasures of Burgundy is its unique
quietness, often accentuated by the
fact that much of the time the villages
seem deserted. Here in the village of
Morey-Saint-Denis I sat and watched
this local family and friends engaged
in a game of *boules*. The afternoon
silence was punctuated by the
satisfying metallic click of the
gleaming spheres, accompanied by
shouts of encouragement and good
humoured arguments concerning the
rules of the game.

CAVE
MOREY
Visitez
D17
2 CHAMB
ROUTE D

Vineyard above Morey-Saint-Denis

In this painting four family groups from the village below are separately tending their own vineyard plots. Here the rows of vines descend steeply to the narrow streets of the village itself, a reminder of how intimately inter-connected is village life with vineyard management. Hardly anyone living in the village is exempt from involvement in one or other aspect of wine production.

Leaving Morey-Saint-Denis, the wine route runs along the sweep of the hills to Chambolle-Musigny, which nestles at the foot of the highest hill in the Côtes de Nuits.

Chambolle-Musigny

This legendary vineyard is alive with activity and chatter. Pausing for a moment in the back-breaking work, a family of farmers stop to gossip and joke as the baskets of their famous fruit lie tumbled around them.

I spent a pleasant evening in a village kitchen at Chambolle-Musigny while the farmer's wife plied me with some delicious side dishes and the husband explained to me with some pride why the wine produced from Le Musigny vineyard is so rare. Owing to a sudden change in soil type, this vineyard and those adjacent to it produce a completely different style of wine to the surrounding villages. Musigny is, as I discovered, silky, lacy, elegant wine – incredibly perfumed. In fact this could be described as the great feminine wine of the Côte de Nuits, as opposed to the masculine power and earthy splendour of the nearby *grand crus* in Gevrey and Morey – silk as opposed to steel.

MMLoxton

The narrow road descends the hill
with a turning right signposted to
the Clos de Vougeot and its fine
Renaissance château with a wine
museum in its huge cellars and
medieval wine presses in the
courtyard.

Clos de Vougeot

Standing proudly amongst its
outstretched lines of famous vines,
the massive monastic château-fort
of Vougeot forms a striking central
point to this view of the Clos de
Vougeot. Its strong lines and
squared rooftops contrast
dramatically with the rows of soft
verdant crops and the animated
figures filling the foreground. A
passer-by seems to have just cycled
up to see how the harvest is going,
stopping to discuss with his
neighbours the prospects for the
new vintage.
The Château de Vougeot and its
Clos is the single most striking
landmark in the Burgundy
countryside of the Côte d'Or.
Although the great Clos is now
split up between a hundred owners,
there is a shared pride in a unique
historic tradition.

From the Clos de Vougeot, the winding road continues along the hillside before finally descending to the village of Vosne-Romanée.

Vosne-Romanée

A farmer calls across to another family to check if they are ready for the tractor to pick up their loaded baskets. This sort of cooperative spirit was not common in previous generations. Many of today's *vignerons* went to the Lycée Viticole de Beaune together, and friendships have been forged between former rival families.

There is little indication that the land surrounding the village of Vosne-Romanée is perhaps the most valuable in Burgundy. This area received much interest when Louis XV's cousin, the Prince de Conti, owned a large area of La Romanée vineyard higher up the hill behind the village. Such royal approval was enhanced when the surgeon Fagon cured Louis XV of a stomach complaint by subscribing Romanée-Saint-Vivant (the vineyard slopes right down to the village) which made these *grand cru* wines essential drinking at court and throughout Paris society. Today they are amongst the most expensive wines in the world.

From Vosne-Romanée there is a
pleasant cycle ride running roughly
parallel to the main route until we
arrive at the bustling town of Nuits-
St-Georges.

Pavement Café, Nuits-St-Georges

At this pavement café, surrounded by
whitewashed shops and a hotel, a
waiter with apron and regulation
waistcoat looks on as a *vigneron* brings
his fist gently down on the table to
accentuate a point to his two
brothers, one a priest. Their
conversation ranges over the quality
of recent vintages, the untrustworthy
late summer weather, the fight against
insect pests and weeds and the
deviousness of the government.

EDEN-CINEMA
HOTEL
BAR D'E
COIFFEUR
CAFÉ DE MARC
CORDONNIER

The Card Game, Nuits-St-Georges

The walls and ceiling of this café are faded and have been stained a rich golden brown by years of smoke from Gaulloise cigarettes. The furniture is rather less pleasant – garish plastic and metal – but the atmosphere is alive and the level of conversation deafening. A poster on the wall announces the Fête du Vin, a fast approaching public holiday.

The two brothers in our picture had entered the café, noisily greeting the proprietor while, without a word, a waiter laid out drinks, a jug of water and a pack of cards at their usual table.

MMLoxton

CAVE
MORE
Visitez
Degusta
200 m
TABAC
COIFFEUR
CA
MMLoxton

Fête du Vin, Nuits-St-Georges

This public holiday, the Fête du Vin, is certainly one of the high points of a journey through the Côte d'Or: crowds dressed in traditional costumes; strings of coloured lights run up between buildings; trestle tables set up with bright red canopies and laid out with all manner of goods from cakes and children's clothing to antiques and books.

Harassed waiters try to cope with overcrowded cafés and makeshift bars selling bottles of wine set up on the other side of the road with barrels as tables. As the three-piece band blares away some couples bob sedately up and down and seem quite unperturbed by others who, with spirited enthusiasm, charge from one side of the road to the other.

The town of Nuits-St-Georges brings us to the end of the Côte de Nuits. Here we leave the vineyards for a while to consider some of my experiences and paintings that in some small way describe varied aspects of the quality of life in Burgundy.

Le Déjeuner

Two farmers take a light lunch of bread and cheese. It is a time for indulging in a few glasses of wine, discussing important local matters and taking a well-earned rest before returning to work.

Market day in Burgundy *(overleaf)*

It is market day and the serious business of life takes place here. These wise people do not eat to live, they live to eat, and whatever the economic climate this ritual must not be disturbed. After all, they make the best wine in the world and it is wholly logical that it should be accompanied by great peasant cooking from the finest ingredients in the region.

The men enjoy a game of *boules* as their wives go about selecting exactly the right ingredients from the market. The region's excellent raw materials are on display: tomatoes, *haricots verts* and aubergines; live chicken, goats, rabbits and pigs; a fabulous range of cheeses; olives and free range eggs; Burgundy's famed cherries, walnuts and almonds.

The stallholder expects no mercy from the Burgundian housewife, and gets none. She prods and squeezes the produce, sniffing and poking suspiciously. It is taken for granted that the goods should be up to her exacting standards: but if they are not, the trader will be told in no uncertain terms. These women are held in high esteem. They not only are discerning buyers but also spend as much of the family income on food as the English do on their cars and hobbies.

M H Loxton

M M Loxton

HOTE

Back from the Market

The nuns give silent thanks for the arrival of such heavenly provisions, while the
pig looks on with some anxiety.

Le Dimanche

A farming family had invited me to Sunday lunch along with a few of their friends. I was the first to arrive, and as I entered the house, assorted goats and chickens were shooed out of the door. Soon the room was filled with friends and relations, inspiring a crossfire of local gossip. However, one by one they came up to me and wanted to know about my visit.

A voice from the kitchen called us to the table, where a large range of dishes and piles of long thin crispy loaves gave little indication of the gastronomic marathon to follow. A fish dish was followed by rabbit roasted with herbs and mustard, followed by boeuf bourguignon – and all accompanied by the most delicious Burgundian wines. After dessert had been consumed and an amazing range of local cheeses nibbled at, coffee and large glasses of *marc* were served outside. I managed to get a sketch of this pleasant afternoon scene before nodding off in a hazy stupor.

Le Coq Blanc

Here the proud farmer's wife holds her champion white Bresse cockerel – one of a much treasured breed peculiar to Burgundy and considered throughout France to be the very finest of table birds. Their breeding is strictly controlled and, in common with the wines of France, is protected by its own *appellation contrôlée*. The exceptional reputation of these fowls was so tarnished by fraudulent early twentieth-century imitations, that such regulations became necessary.

MMLoxton

After leaving Nuits-St-Georges we cycled along the hillside route past famous
vineyards until we joined the main route after the vineyard Les St-Georges. It was
not long before we came to the turning for Aloxe-Corton, lying snugly below the
hill of Corton.

The great sweep of the hill dramatically announces the Côte de Beaune, the
area covering the second half of my journey.

Maison Latour Press House

The Press House at Château Corton Grancey, and its surrounding *grand cru*
vineyard form the jewel in the crown of the great *négociant-éleveur*, Louis Latour.
Here we see château workers bringing in the harvest in baskets whose design is
unique to Maison Latour. Below the densely wooded summit of the hill at
Corton, following the sweep of the hill is the largest *grand cru* vineyard in
Burgundy; first planted by the Emperor Charlemagne at the end of the eighth
century AD. Corton was one of the Emperor's favourite wines, but when first
planted, produced only red wine. As he grew older, and his great beard whiter, red
wine stains began to appear, alarming the Empress who was concerned for her
husband's reputation and ascetic appearance as Holy Roman Emperor. A brilliant
solution was found with the replanting of an area of Corton for white wine
production; the new vineyard was named Corton-Charlemagne, producing a
masculine and complex wine, eminently suitable for the medieval banquet table
of princes.

MM Loxton

The Cellarman, Maison Latour

A young Englishman at Latour's office in Beaune had, with great enthusiasm,
organized a visit for me to the famous cellars below the Press House. The head
cellarman from Château Grancey guided me past wagons laden with grapes which
were being unloaded at a frantic pace, and then through a heavy door leading to a
dark vestibule. As the door was closed, shutting out the late summer heat, I
caught the pleasing musty smell of fermented grapes in the air. Passing down the
racks of fine wines covered in a cobweb-like growth which thrives on wine fumes
and the damp atmosphere, this cellarman took me through an agreeably amusing
history lesson on the vintages of the nineteenth and twentieth centuries and the
great men who drank them, from Napoleon to Pompidou. We tasted great wines
in these convivial, murky surroundings for two hours.

Walled Vineyard, Aloxe-Corton

In the background of this picture can be seen the château of Corton-André in the
village of Aloxe-Corton. With its handsome gilded mosaic roof it is one of the
finest examples of Burgundian architecture. The Château forms the headquarters
of the wine business of Pierre André, grower and *négociant* on the largest scale,
and stands at the heart of a 105-acre estate, producing red and white wine of
international repute.

Descending the narrow road from Aloxe-Corton we then took the main road into the medieval town of Beaune, the capital of the Côte D'Or.

Hôtel Dieu: Hospices de Beaune

In this scene, members of the brotherhood of the Chevaliers du Tastevin march in worshipful procession, beneath the steep, brightly coloured, tiled roof of the Hôtel-Dieu, at the start of a celebratory weekend of drinking and feasting. (The brotherhood was founded in the 1930s to represent all the region's wine growers and producers, rather than any particular private interests.)

Until the Duke of Burgundy moved to Dijon in the fourteenth century, Beaune was in all respects the Burgundian capital. Medieval in atmosphere, the old walled town is rich in architectural reminders of its glorious past. Under the town is a vast labyrinth of medieval passages and cellars. In the town centre is the magnificent Hôtel-Dieu of the Hospices de Beaune, founded in 1443 by Nicolas Rolin, Chancellor of Philip the Good, Duke of Burgundy (who is himself notorious for having sold Joan of Arc to Henry IV of England). This charitable institution, whose purpose is to relieve the region's poor and sick, raises its money by annual November wine auctions.

As we left the main route from Beaune we forked right along small side roads
passing vineyards of little note until rising ground signalled the approach of the
village of Pommard.

Clos de la Commaraine, Pommard

The wine harvesters of the Clos de la Commaraine all work for the château of the
same name. Built on medieval foundations, retaining its original twelfth-century
cellars, this château produces a full-bodied, succulent red burgundy, much
favoured by American wine afficionados.
　　To my great regret, in spite of considerable planning, it was necessary to cycle
straight through the next village, Volnay, without time to make sketches owing to
a pressing engagement with a farmer in Meursault. I will certainly return to
sketch the fine mansions and imposing courtyards of this well-kept village.

Château de Meursault

This vineyard is situated on the site of the old gardens of the château, but the potential of this land to produce wine of outstanding quality proved irresistible to the owner.

The imposing seventeenth-century Château de Meursault now hosts the annual feast of La Paulée, which takes place on the same November weekend as the wine auction at the Hospices de Beaune. In contrast to the formal grandeur of the Beaune celebrations, the Paulée de Meursault is an authentically earthy village party for the local *vignerons* and their friends. Each family brings along wine from its cellars for the enjoyment of one and all.

MM loxton

The Town Square, Meursault

At a café opposite the great landmark
of the town hall of Meursault, during
one of the numerous saints' days, I
took the opportunity to observe, and
attempt to understand, the finer
points of *boules*, a game I had
encountered innumerable times
during my travels through the Côte
d'Or. It was obviously a game of skill
and dexterity, rather than physical
effort, and I must thank one of the
waiters for explaining the details.
Each player has three steel *boules*,
identified by different etched patterns.
At the beginning of each round, a
small wooden ball, the *cochonnet*, or
jack, is tossed all the way up the
playing area. At the round's end, the
player with the *boule* closest to the
cochonnet is the winner.

Firstly, it seems obligatory that the
player unfailingly taps the spheres
together, then in a crouched position,
takes hold of the *boule*, fingers curled
downwards. When it is thrown,
friction from the finger action
provides necessary backspin. Amongst
many variations two basic shots can
be identified: the low-trajectory throw
that skids along the dusty ground well
before closing on the *cochonnet*, and
the high drop shot, aimed to knock
the opponent's closest *boule* out of the
way. These throws are delivered with
great skill – especially when
accompanied by all manner of
grunting and shouts of
encouragement to help the shot on
its way.

From Mersault we rode along quiet lanes to the picturesque village of Puligny Montrachet whose vineyards produce the best white wines in Burgundy.

Inspecting the grapes, Puligny

Many generations of *vignerons* in Burgundy have passed on the experience and wisdom gained by tireless experimentation. It became evident to me that many of the younger growers that I met who went to wine school hold some of the older generation in high esteem. What they lack in scientific knowledge and learning is clearly more than compensated for by cumulative experience. Questions of quality, and the quantity of grapes to be produced from each row of vines, and exactly when they should be picked, are largely a matter of instinct derived from great experience.

Here a peasant *vigneron* inspects the condition of the grapes in a row of inherited vines. Keeping in mind the weather conditions, he will decide whether or not picking is to begin. His wife and daughters wait in readiness.

From Puligny there is a short cycle ride to the hillside village of Chassagne
Montrachet with its steep streets and fine old buildings.

Chassange Montrachet

From an elevated viewpoint in this charming village I was impressed by the
remarkably untouched medieval architecture and the variegated brown hues of the
weathered stone and brickwork.

MMLoxton

Going Home

The grape harvest ends with all sorts of festivities, from a single communal meal
to more formal fêtes. Here it is traditional on the last day of harvest, for the grape
pickers to accompany the final cartload of grapes back to the cellar or place of
vinification, where drinks will be served to celebrate another successful vintage.

Acknowledgements

To Stanley Harries of RONA Gallery, Mayfair, London for first encouraging me to visit the Côte D'Or in Burgundy;

to the local people of Burgundy who showed great kindness and understanding to one who knew so little of their rich inheritance, customs and ways;

to Peter Willis of Wine Arts, Andover for bringing my paintings of Burgundy to a wider audience in limited edition prints;

and finally, to my husband Stan who accompanied me on this journey and was endlessly supportive.